MYTHICAL
BEASTS

*An Anthology of
Verse & Prose*

MYTHICAL
BEASTS

An Anthology of
Verse & Prose

SMITHMARK

© Anness Publishing Limited 1996

All rights reserved. No part of this publication may be
reproduced, stored in a retrieval system, or transmitted in
any way or by any means, electronic, mechanical,
photocopying, recording or otherwise, without the prior
written permission of the copyright holder.

This edition published in 1996 by
Smithmark Publishers, a division of U.S. Media Holdings, Inc.,
16 East 32nd Street,
New York,
NY 10016.

SMITHMARK books are available for bulk purchase for sales
promotion and for premium use. For details write or call
the manager of special sales, SMITHMARK Publishers Inc.
16 East 32nd Street, New York, 10016; (212) 532-6600

Produced by Anness Publishing Limited
1 Boundary Row
London SE1 8HP

Printed and bound in Singapore by Star Standard Industries Pte. Ltd.

10 9 8 7 6 5 4 3 2 1

Contents

ℐNTRODUCTION

~ ✦ ~

Monstrous beasts play an important role in every mythology. Giant predators like the dragon or the roc, hybrids like the griffin or the sphinx, and half-human creatures such as satyrs, centaurs and harpies, have gripped the human imagination for thousands of years. Humans, it seems, love to be frightened, or at least need a physical expression of their nightmares. Either way, artists and story-tellers have explored these fantasies to spine-tingling effect.

Not that all mythical beasts are monsters. Pegasus, the winged horse, is a peaceful and playful creature; and the unicorn, while fierce and untamable – except through its fatal attraction to innocent girls – has come to symbolize a lost paradise. Nor are many of the mythical beasts in this collection likely to have had much, if any, basis in fact. But if they are mostly products of the imagination, the expression of our darkest fears, they are no less fascinating for that. As John Aubrey wrote in the seventeenth century, "Old customs and old wives fables are grosse things but 'tis a pleasure to consider the Errors that enveloped former ages, as also at present." The current obsession with horror of every kind, in books and films, merely goes to show that the pleasurable shudder induced by contemplation of the Beast, both within us and without, is a timeless one.

THE BASILISK
or Cockatrice

This animal was called the king of the serpents. In confirmation of his royalty he was said to be endowed with a crest, or comb upon the head, constituting a crown. He was supposed to be produced from the egg of a cock hatched under toads or serpents. There were several species of this animal. One species burned up whatever they approached; a second were a kind of wandering Medusa's heads, and their look caused an instant horror which was immediately followed by death. In Shakespeare's play of "Richard the Third" Lady Anne, in answer to Richard's compliment on her eyes, says, *"Would they were basilisk's, to strike thee dead!"*

The basilisks were called kings of serpents because all other serpents and snakes fled the moment they heard the distant hiss of their king, although they might be occupied upon the most delicious prey, the sole enjoyment of which they would leave to the royal monster.

The Roman naturalist Pliny thus describes him: *"He does not impel his body, like other serpents, by a multiplied flexion, but advances lofty and upright. He kills the shrubs, not only by contact, but by breathing on them, and splits the rocks, such power of evil is there in him."* It was formerly believed that if killed by a spear from on horseback the power of the poison conducted through the weapon killed not only the rider, but the horse also.

THOMAS BULFINCH, THE AGE OF FABLE

CENTAURS

~ ❦ ~

So Tiphys the helmsman steered them to the shore under the crags of Pelion; and they went up through the dark pine forests towards the Centaur's cave... and Achilles brought him his harp; and he began a wondrous song; a famous story of old time, of the fight between the Centaurs and the Lapithai, which you may still see carved in stone. He sang how his brothers came to ruin by their folly, when they were mad with wine; and how they and the heroes fought, with fists, and teeth, and the goblets from which they drank; and how they tore up the pine-trees in their fury, and hurled great crags of stone, while the mountains thundered with the battle, and the land was wasted far and wide; till the Lapithai drove them from their home in the rich Thessalian plains to the lonely glens of Pindus, leaving Cheiron all alone. And the heroes praised his song right heartily; for some of them had helped in that great fight.

CHARLES KINGSLEY, THE HEROES

10

CHEIRON THE CENTAUR

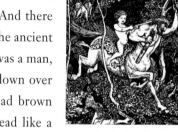

The lad went in without trembling, for he too was a hero's son; but when he was within, he stopped in wonder to listen to that magic song. And there he saw the singer lying upon bearskins and fragrant boughs: Cheiron, the ancient centaur, the wisest of all things beneath the sky. Down to the waist he was a man, but below he was a noble horse; his white hair rolled down over his broad shoulders, and his white beard over his broad brown chest; and his eyes were wise and mild, and his forehead like a mountain-wall. And in his hands he held a harp of gold, and struck it with a golden key; and as he struck, he sang till his eyes glittered, and filled all the cave with light. And he sang of the birth of Time, and of the heavens and the dancing stars; and of the ocean, and the ether, and the fire, and the shaping of the wondrous earth. And he sang of the treasures of the hills, and of the hidden jewels of the mine, and the veins of fire and metal, and the virtues of all healing herbs, and of the speech of birds, and of prophecy, and of hidden things to come.

CHARLES KINGSLEY, THE HEROES

CERBERUS
12th Labour of Hercules

~ ❖ ~

Down in the underworld was a three-headed dog named Cerberus, and round each of his heads was a mane of writhing snakes, while his tail was a huge serpent. Moreover, Cerberus was as large as an elephant, and any mortal who dared to cross the river Styx was torn to pieces by this dread guardian of the land of whispers.

Pluto and Proserpine received Hercules kindly; he was a mortal whose fame had spread even to the lower world, and knowing that the gods had decreed the servitude of the hero who had never failed in any mission on which Eurystheus had sent him, Pluto, when Hercules told him why he had come to the underworld, agreed to allow him to take Cerberus to earth on condition that it was done without force of arms.

This meant that Hercules must not hurt the giant monster, whose three heads were poison-fanged, and every strand of whose mane was a writhing poisonous snake! But Hercules did not mind what restrictions were placed upon him; he had come to take the dog to the light of day, and take him he would.

So he fastened the monster with a great chain, and in spite of the bitings and snappings of the dog, which roared out with anger at being handled in such a manner, Hercules began to drag Cerberus through the shadow-land. The thunderous roll of the voices of Cerberus echoed and echoed through the cavernous depths, but Hercules took no notice of the roarings or of the snappings. He kept on with his hauling, drawing nearer and nearer the upper world, until at last the full blaze of day was reached.

Christine Chaundler and Eric Wood,
The Labours of Hercules

14

THE CHIMAERA

Echidna bore Chimaera, whose breath was raging fire, terrible and mighty, swift of foot and strong. And she had three heads: one the head of a fierce-eyed lion, the other of a goat, the third of a snake, even a mighty dragon. In front she was a lion, behind a dragon, in the midst a goat, breathing the terrible might of blazing fire...

HESIOD, THEOGONY

There seemed to be a heap of strange and terrible creatures curled up within the cavern. Their bodies lay so close together that Bellerophon could not distinguish them apart; but, judging by their heads, one of these creatures was a huge snake, the second a fierce lion, and the third an ugly goat. The lion and the goat were asleep; the snake was broad awake, and kept staring around him with a great pair of fiery eyes. But – and this was the most wonderful part of the matter – the three spires of smoke evidently issued from the nostrils of these three heads! So strange was the spectacle that, though Bellerophon had been all along expecting it, the truth did not immediately occur to him that here was the terrible three-headed Chimaera. He had found out the Chimaera's cavern! The snake, the lion, and the goat, as he supposed them to be, were not three separate creatures, but one monster!

NATHANIEL HAWTHORNE, TANGLEWOOD TALES

CYCLOPS

~ ❖ ~

The Cyclopes were giants, who inhabited an island of which they were the only possessors. The name means *"round eye"*, and these giants were so called because they had but one eye, and that placed in the middle of the forehead. They dwelt in caves and fed on the wild productions of the island and on what their flocks yielded, for they were shepherds. Ulysses left the main body of his ships at anchor, and with one vessel went to the Cyclopes' island to explore for supplies. He landed with his companions, carrying with them a jar of wine for a present, and coming to a large cave they entered it, and finding no one within examined its contents. They found it stored with the richest of the flock, quantities of cheese, pails and bowls of milk, lambs and kids in their pens, all in nice order. Presently arrived the master of the  cave, Polyphemus, bearing an immense bundle of firewood, which he threw down before the cavern's mouth. He then drove into the cave the sheep and goats to be milked, and, entering, rolled to the cave's mouth an enormous rock, that twenty oxen could not draw. Next he sat down and milked his ewes, preparing a part for cheese, and setting the rest aside for his customary drink. Then, turning round his great eye, he discerned the strangers, and growled out to them, demanding who they were, and where from.

Thomas Bulfinch, The Age of Fable

DRAGONS

~ ❖ ~

So deeply associated was the dragon with the popular legends, that we find stories of encounters with it passing down into the literature of the Middle Ages; and, like the heroes of old, the Christian saints won their principal renown by dragon achievements. Thus among the dragon-slayers we find that St Phillip the Apostle destroyed a huge dragon at Hieropolis in Phrygia. St Martha killed the terrible dragon called Tarasque at Aix *(la Chapelle)*. St Florent killed a similar dragon which haunted the Loire. St Cado, St Maudet, and St Paul did similar feats in Brittany. St Keyne of Cornwall slew a dragon. St Michael, St George, St Margaret, Pope Sylvester, St Samson, Archbishop of Dol, Donatus *(fourth century)*, St Clement of Metz, killed dragons. And St Romain from Rouen destroyed the huge dragon called La Gargouille, which ravaged the Seine.

CHARLES GOULD, MYTHICAL MONSTERS

GORGONS

Straight downward, two or three thousand feet below him, Perseus perceived a small island, with the sea breaking into white foam all around its rocky shore, except on one side, where there was a beach of snowy sand. He descended towards it, and, looking earnestly at a cluster or heap of brightness at the foot of a precipice of black rocks, behold, there were the terrible Gorgons! They lay fast asleep, soothed by the thunder of the sea; for it required a tumult that would have deafened everybody else to lull such fierce creatures into slumber.

The moonlight glistened on their steely scales, and on their golden wings, which drooped idly over the sand. Their brazen claws, horrible to look at, were thrust out, and clutched the wave-beaten fragments of rock, while the sleeping Gorgons dreamed of tearing some poor mortal all to pieces. The snakes that served them instead of hair seemed likewise to be asleep, although now and then one would writhe, and lift its head, and thrust out its forked tongue, emitting a drowsy hiss, and then let itself subside among its sister snakes.

NATHANIEL HAWTHORNE,
TANGLEWOOD TALES

MEDUSA THE GORGON

As he was fully aware of Medusa's petrifying proclivities, he advanced very cautiously, holding his shield before him at such an angle that all surrounding objects were clearly reflected on its smooth, mirrorlike surface.

He thus discovered Medusa asleep, raised his sword, and, without looking at anything but her mirrored form, severed her head from her body, seized it in one hand, and, holding it persistently behind his back, flew away in great haste, lest the two remaining Gorgons should fall upon him and attempt to avenge their sister's death.

Perseus then swiftly winged his way over land and sea, carefully holding his ghastly trophy behind him; and as he flew, Medusa's blood trickled down on the hot African sand, where it gave birth to a race of poisonous reptiles destined to infest the region in future ages, and cause the death of many an adventurous explorer. The drops which fell into the sea were utilised by Neptune, who created from them the famous winged steed called Pegasus.

H.A. GUERBER, THE MYTHS OF GREECE AND ROME

GRIFFINS

~ ❖ ~

In that Contree *(the land of Bacharie)* ben many Griffounes, more plentee than in ony Contree. Sum men seyn that thei hand the Body upward as an Egle, and benethe as a Lyoun: and treuly thei seyn sothe, that thei ben of that schapp. But a Griffoun hathe the body more gret and is more strong thanne 8 Lyouns; and more gret and strong than an 100 Egles, such as we han amonges us. For a Griffoun wil bere, fleynge to his Nest, a gret Horse, or 2 Oxen yoked togider, as thei gon at the Plowghe. For he hathe his Talouns so longe and so large and grete upon his Feet. as thoughe thei weren Hornes of grete Oxen; so that men maken Cuppes of hem, to drynken of; and of her Ribbes and of the Pennes of hir Wenges, men maken Bowes fulle stronge, to schote with Arwes and Quarelle.

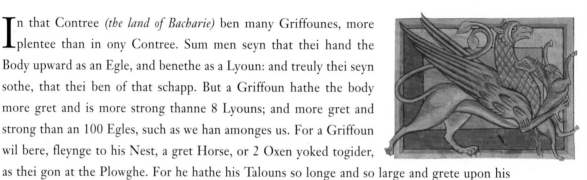

Sir John Mandeville, Travels

As for the testimonie of ancient writers, they are but derivative, and terminate all in one Aristeus, a poet of Proconesus, who affirmed that near the Arimaspi, or one-eyed nation, griffins defended the mines of gold.

Sir Thomas Browne, Pseudodoxia Epidemica

HARPIES

O nce when they had landed to rest awhile upon a lonely shore, they spread out a meal for themselves; but no sooner had they done so than their food was snatched away from them by the Harpies – three dreadful monsters, half women and half birds – who suddenly swooped down upon them. Being very hungry, the wanderers spread out a second meal; and when the Harpies again drew near, they managed to beat them off. But one of the horrid monsters perched on a rock and croaked out a dismal prophecy of ill-luck, declaring that though in the end they would reach the country promised to them they would first have many more dreadful hardships to go through and at one time would have to endure a terrible famine, when they would be so hungry that they would be glad to chew pieces of wood and would be nearly starved to death.

GLADYS DAVIDSON, THE WANDERINGS OF AENEAS

Of monsters all, most monstrous this; no greater wrath
God sends 'mongst men; it comes from depth of pitchy Hell:
And Virgin's face, but wombe-like gulfe unsatiate hath,
Her hands are griping clawes, her colour pale and fell.

VIRGIL

For now, indeed, the trembling Minyae
Beheld the daughters of the earth and sea,
The dreadful snatchers, who like women were
Down to the breast, with scanty coarse black hair
About their heads, and dim eyes ringed with red,
And bestial mouths set round with lips of lead,
But from their gnarled necks
there began to spring
Half hair, half feathers, and
a sweeping wing
Grew out instead of arm on
either side,
And thick plumes underneath
the breast did hide
The place where joined the
fearful natures twain.

Grey feathered were they else, with many a stain
Of blood thereon, and on birds' claws they went.
These through the hall unheard-of shrieking sent,
And rushed at Phineus, just as to his mouth
He raised the golden cup to quench his drouth,
And scattered the red wine, and buffeted

The wretched king, and one,
perched on his head,
Laughed as the furies laugh

WILLIAM MORRIS, THE LIFE
AND DEATH OF JASON

THE JABBERWOCKY

Twas brillig, and the slithy toves
Did gyre and gimble in the wabe:
All mimsy were the borogroves,
And the mome raths outgrabe.

"Beware the Jabberwock, my son!
The jaws that bite, the claws that catch!
Beware the Jubjub bird, and shun
The frumious Bandersnatch!"

He took his vorpal sword in hand:
Long time the manxome foe he sought
So rested he by the Tumtum tree,
And stood awhile in thought.

And as in uffish thought he stood,
The Jabberwock, with eyes of flame,
Came whiffling through the tulgey wood,
And burbled as it came!

One, two! One, two! And through and through
The vorpal blade went snicker-snack!
He left it dead, and with its head
He went galumphing back.

"And hast thou slain the Jabberwock?
Come to my arms, my beamish boy!
O frabjous day! Callooh! Callay!"
He chortled in his joy.

Twas brillig, and the slithy toves
Did gyre and gimble in the wabe:
All mimsy were the borogroves,
And the mome raths outgrabe.

LEWIS CARROLL, JABBERWOCKY

MERMAIDS & MERMEN

To sea, to sea! The calm is o'er;
  The wanton water leaps in sport,
And rattles down the pebbly shore;
  The dolphin wheels, the sea-cows snort,
And unseen mermaids' pearly song
Comes bubbling up, the weeds among.
  Fling broad the sail, dip deep the oar:
  To sea, to sea! The calm is o'er.

THOMAS LOVELL BEDDOES, SAILOR'S SONG

THE 𝕸INOTAUR

And when the evening came, the guards came in and led Theseus away to the labyrinth. And he went down into that doleful gulf, through winding paths among the rocks, under caverns, and arches, and galleries, and over heaps of fallen stone. And he turned on the left hand, and on the right hand, and went up and down, till his head was dizzy; but all the while he held his clue. For when he went in he had fastened it to a stone, and left it to unroll out of his hand as he went on; and it lasted him till he met the Minotaur, in a narrow chasm between black cliffs.

And when he saw him he stopped awhile, for he had never seen so strange a beast. His body was a man's: but his head was the head of a bull; and his teeth were the teeth of a lion; and with them he tore his prey. And when he saw Theseus he roared, and put his head down, and rushed right at him. But Theseus stepped aside nimbly, and as he passed by, cut him in the knee; and ere he could turn in the narrow path, he followed him, and stabbed him again and again from behind, till the monster fled bellowing wildly; for he never before had felt a wound. And Theseus followed him at full speed, holding the clue of thread in his left hand.

Then on, through cavern after cavern, under dark ribs of sounding stone, and up rough glens and torrent-beds, among the sunless roots of Ida, and to the edge of the eternal snow, went they, the hunter and the hunted, while the hills bellowed to the monster's bellow.

Charles Kingsley, The Heroes

THE NEMEAN LION
1st Labour of Hercules

~ ❧ ~

Many were the wonderful deeds done by Hercules; and the most famous of them all are known as "The Labours of Hercules". In order that this great hero might prove himself fit to dwell on Mount Olympus, the gods commanded that he should offer himself as a slave for twelve years to Eurystheus, King of Mycenae, who, they knew, would set him tasks that seemed impossible and which would require all his mighty strength and bravery to perform.

Hercules was first of all commanded to kill the Nemean lion, a terribly fierce and huge beast that dwelt in the forests of Nemea and which came out at dusk to devour the shepherds and country folk of that part. This lion was believed to have dropped out of the moon; and, being a magical beast, of course it could not be harmed by any weapon made on the earth. Knowing this, Hercules flung away his sword, his bow and arrows, and the immense club he carried; and when the ramping, roaring lion sprang upon him, he bravely seized it in his own powerful hands and strangled the life out of it as he had crushed the serpents when he was a baby. Having thus killed the fierce lion by means of his own mighty strength, he stripped off its fine skin, which he afterwards wore as his chief garment.

GLADYS DAVIDSON, THE LABOURS OF HERCULES

ᴘEGASUS

~ ✦ ~

Bridle in hand, Bellerophon stood pondering her words, until he remembered that Pegasus was a wonderful winged steed, born from the blood which fell into the foam of the sea from Medusa's severed head. This horse, as white as snow, and gifted with immortal life as well as incredible speed, was the favourite mount of Apollo and the Muses, who delighted in taking aerial flights on his broad back; and Bellerophon knew that from time to time he came down to earth to drink of the cool waters of the Hippocrene (a fountain which had bubbled forth where his hooves first touched the earth), or to visit the equally limpid spring of Pirene, near Corinth. Bellerophon therefore proceeded to the latter fountain...

H.A. GUERBER,
THE MYTHS OF GREECE AND ROME

PEGASUS

Nearer and nearer came the aerial wonder, flying in great circles, as you may have seen a dove when about to alight. Downward came Pegasus, in those wide-sweeping circles, which grew narrower and narrower still as he gradually approached the earth. The nigher the view of him, the more beautiful he was, and the more marvellous was the sweep of his silvery wings. At last, with so light a pressure as hardly to bend the grass about the fountain, or to imprint a hoof-tramp in the sand of its margin, he alighted, and, stooping his wild head, began to drink.

At length – not that he was weary, but only idle and luxurious – Pegasus folded his wings, and lay down on the soft green turf. But, being too full of aerial life to remain quiet for many moments together, he soon rolled over on his back with his four slender legs in the air. It was beautiful to see him, this one solitary creature, whose mate had never been created, but who needed no companion, and, living a great many hundred years, was as happy as the centuries were long. Bellerophon and the child almost held their breath, partly from a delightful awe, but still more because they dreaded lest the slightest stir or murmur should send him up, with the speed of an arrow-flight, into the farthest blue of the sky.

Finally, when he had had enough of rolling over and over, Pegasus turned himself about, and indolently, like any other horse, put out his fore-legs in order to rise from the ground; and Bellerophon, who had guessed that he would do so, darted suddenly from the thicket and leaped astride of his back.

NATHANIEL HAWTHORNE,
TANGLEWOOD TALES

THE PHOENIX

Most beings spring from other individuals; but there is a certain kind which reproduces itself. The Assyrians call it the Phoenix. It does not live on fruit or flowers, but on frankincense and odiferous gums. When it has lived five hundred years, it builds itself a nest in the branches of an oak, or on the top of a palm tree. In this it collects cinnamon, and spikenard, and myrrh, and of these materials builds a pile on which it deposits itself, and, dying, breathes out its last breath amidst odours. From the body of the parent bird a young Phoenix issues forth, destined to live as long a life as its predecessor. When this has grown up and gained sufficient strength, it lifts its nest from the tree *(its own cradle and its parent's sepulchre)*, and carries it to the city of Heliopolis in Egypt, and deposits it in the temple of the Sun.

OVID, METAMORPHOSES

THE PHOENIX

It is exceedingly rare and visits the land of Egypt (*as I was told at Heliopolis*) only at intervals of five hundred years, upon the death of the parent bird. Its plumage, judging from paintings, is partly gold and partly red, while in shape and size it resembles the eagle. This is the story they relate of the Phoenix: it brings its parent all the way from Arabia enclosed in a lump of myrrh and buries the body in the temple of the Sun. In order to do this it shapes a quantity of myrrh into the form of an egg as large as it can conveniently carry. It then hollows out the lump, places the parent bird inside, and covers the hole with more myrrh. That done, it carries the egg to the temple of the Sun in Egypt. I tell the story as it was told to me, but I confess I do not believe it.

HERODOTUS, HISTORIES

So when the new-born Phoenix first is seen
Her feathered subjects all adore their queen,
And while she makes her progress through the East,
From every grove her numerous train's increased;
Each poet of the air her glory sings,
And round him the pleased audience clap their wings.

JOHN DRYDEN

ℜOCS

We arrived one day at a large island, deserted and desolate, but on it was an enormous white dome, of great bulk, and, lo, it was the egg of a Roc. When the merchants had landed to amuse themselves, not knowing that it was the egg of a Roc, they struck it with stones, so that it broke, and there poured from it a great quantity of liquid, and the young Roc appeared within the shell. The merchants pulled it out, killed it, and cut from it an abundance of meat. I was then in the ship, and knew not of it, and, looking forth, I saw the merchants striking the egg. I called out to them, *"Do not this deed! It is a Roc's egg, and the bird will come and demolish our ship and destroy us!"* But they would not hear my words.

Suddenly the sun was veiled, and the day grew dark, and we raised our eyes, and, lo, the wings of the Roc darkened the sky! When the bird came and beheld its egg broken it cried out fiercely, whereupon its mate, the female bird, came to it, and they flew in circles over the ship, uttering cries like thunder.

THE STORY OF SINDBAD THE SAILOR

In a few minutes the Roc appeared, and bore me off to the top of the mountain in his huge claws as lightly as if I had been a feather, for this great bird is so strong that he has been known to carry even an elephant to his nest in the hills.

THE ARABIAN NIGHTS

SATYRS

~ ❧ ~

The male divinities of the woods, which were also very numerous, were mostly Satyrs, curious beings with a man's body and a goat's legs, hair and horns. They were all passionately fond of music and revelry, and were wont to indulge in dancing at all times and in all places. The most famous among all the Satyrs was Silenus, Bacchus's tutor; and Pan, or Consentes, god of the shepherds, and the personification of nature. The latter was the reputed son of Mercury and a charming young nymph named Penelope; and we are told that, when his mother first beheld him, she was aghast, for he was the most extraordinary little creature she had ever seen. His body was covered with hair, and his feet and ears were those of a goat.

H.A. GUERBER, THE MYTHS OF GREECE AND ROME

48

PAN THE SATYR

Pan was equally devoted to music, the dance, and pretty nymphs. He saw one of the nymphs, whose name was Syrinx, whom he immediately loved; but unfortunately for him, she, frightened at his appearance, fled. Exasperated by her persistent avoidance of him, Pan once pursued and was about to overtake her, when she paused, and implored Gaea to protect her. The prayer was scarcely ended, when she found herself changed into a clump of reeds, which the panting lover embraced, thinking he had at last caught the maiden, who had stood in that very spot just a few moments before.

His deception and disappointment were so severe that they wrung from him a prolonged sigh, which, passing through the rustling reeds, produced plaintive tones. Pan, seeing Syrinx had gone for ever, took seven pieces of the reed, of unequal lengths, bound them together, and fashioned from them a musical instrument

H.A. GUERBER, THE MYTHS OF GREECE AND ROME

Fair, trembling Syrinx fled *Naught but a lovely sighing of the wind*
Arcadian Pan, with such a fearful dread. *Along the reedy stream; a half-heard strain*
Poor nymph! poor Pan! how he did weep to find *Full of sweet desolation; balmy pain.*

KEATS

Scylla

~ ❦ ~

In the midst of this cliff is a cave wherein dwelleth Scylla, the dreadful monster of the sea. Her voice is but as the voice of a whelp newly born, and her twelve feet are small and ill-grown, but she hath six necks, exceeding long, and on each a head dreadful to behold, and in each head three rows of teeth, thick set and full of death. She is hidden up to her middle in the cave, but she putteth her heads out of it, fishing for dolphins, or sea-dogs, or other creatures of the sea, for indeed there are countless flocks of them. No ship can pass her by unharmed, for with each head she carrieth off a man, snatching them from the ship's deck. Hard by, even a bow-shot off, is the other rock, lower by far, and with a great fig tree growing on the top. Beneath it Charybdis thrice a day sucketh in the water, and thrice a day spouteth it forth. If thou chance to be there when she sucks it in, not even Poseidon's help could save thee. See, therefore, that thou guide thy ship near to Scylla rather than to the other, for it is better for thee to lose six men out of thy ship, than all thy company together.

A.J. Church, The Story of the Odyssey

SIRENS

~ ❧ ~

A nd first I told them of the Sirens; and while I spake we came to the Sirens' island. Then did the breeze cease, and there was a windless calm. So my comrades took down the sails and put out the oars, and I cleft a great round of wax with my sword, and, melting it in the sun, I anointed therewith the ears of my men; afterwards they bound me by hands and feet, as I stood upright by the mast. And when we were so near the shore as that the shout of a man could be heard therefrom, the Sirens perceived the ship, and began their song. And their song was this:

Hither, Ulysses, great Achaian name, Turn thy swift keel, and listen to our lay;
Since never pilgrim near these regions came, In black ship on the azure fields astray,
But heard our sweet voice ere he sailed away, And in his joy passed on with ampler mind.
We know what labours were in ancient day Wrought in wide Troia, as the gods assigned;
We know from land to land all toils of all mankind.

A.J. CHURCH, THE STORY OF THE ODYSSEY

THE SPHINX

While listening to these tidings, of a terrible monster called the Sphinx, Oedipus saw a herald pass along the street, proclaiming that the throne and the queen's hand would be the reward of any man who dared encounter the Sphinx and was fortunate enough to free the country of its terrible presence. He resolved to slay the dreaded monster, and, with that purpose in view, advanced slowly, sword in hand, along the road where lurked the Sphinx. He soon found the monster, which from afar propounded the following enigma,warning him, at the same time, that he forfeited his life if he failed to give the correct answer. "Tell me, what animal it is that has four feet at morning bright, has two at noon, and three at night?"

Oedipus was not devoid of intelligence, by any manner of means, and soon concluded that the animal could only be man, who in infancy, when too weak to stand, creeps along on hands and knees, in manhood walks wrect, and in old age supports his tottering steps with a staff. This reply, evidently as correct as unexpected, was received by the Sphinx with a hoarse cry of disappointment and rage as it turned to fly; but ere it could effect its purpose, it was stayed by Oedipus, who drove it at his sword's point over the edge of the precipice, where it was killed.

H.A. GUERBER, THE MYTHS OF GREECE AND ROME

THE STYMPHALIAN BIRDS
5th Labour of Hercules

~ ✤ ~

These birds had brazen beaks and claws and wings, and they would swoop down, kill any whom they saw, and devour them! They were, indeed a terrible pest, and no one could drive them away from the marsh where they had taken refuge.

Hercules, after having inspected the marsh, which he saw was literally covered by the birds, realised that he was face to face with a very difficult task, and that unless he received help, he could not possibly succeed.

Help came to him from his friend, the goddess Minerva, who gave him a great horn rattle with instructions how to use it. That was indeed a very queer sort of weapon with which to fight the birds, but it was a very effective one. Hercules went up on to the top of a mountain near the marsh and, standing there, shook his rattle with all his might. Such a noise it made! The people in the neighbourhood put their fingers in their ears to deaden the sound; and the birds in the swamp, startled as they had never been before, left their resting-places and rose high in the air – a great swarm which hid the light of the sun!

This was just what Hercules had expected. He drew his bow, and shot his poisoned arrows at the birds. Hercules had never shot so rapidly in his life as he did now, and great numbers of the wild birds fell to the ground dead. Those which escaped flew on and on, and never again did they dare go near the swamp.

Christine Chaundler and Eric Wood, The Labours of Hercules

Unicorns

~ ❧ ~

These Beasts are very swift, and their legges have no Articles *(joints)*. They keep for the most part in the deserts, and live solitary in the tops of the Mountaines. There was nothing more horrible than the voice or braying of it, for the voice is strain'd above measure. It fighteth both with the mouth and with the heeles, with the mouth biting like a Lyon and with the heeles kicking like a Horse. It is sayd that Unicorns above all other creatures doe reverence Virgines and young Maides, and that many times at the sight of them they grow tame, and come and sleepe beside them, for there is in their nature a certaine savor, wherewithall the Unicornes are allured and delighted; for which occasion the Indian and Ethiopian hunters use this strategem to take the beast.

Edward Topsell, The Historie of Foure-footed Beastes

Unicorns

~ ❧ ~

Lo! in the mute, mid wilderness,
What wondrous Creature?
of no kind!
His burning lair doth largely press
Gaze fixt and feeding on the wind?
His fell is of the desert dye,
And tissue adust, dun-yellow and dry,
Compact of living sands; his eye
Black luminary, soft and mild,
With its dark lustre cools the wild;
From his stately forehead springs
Piercing to heaven, a radiant horn,
Lo! the compeer of lion-kings!
The steed self-armed, the Unicorn!
Ever heard of, never seen,
With a main of sands between
Him and approach; his lonely pride
To course his arid arena wide,
Free as the hurricane, or lie here
Lord of his couch as his career!
Wherefore should this foot profane

His sanctuary, still domain?
Let me turn, ere eye so bland
Perchance be fire-shot, like heaven's
brand,
To whither my boldness! Northward
now,

Behind the white star on his brow
Glittering straight against the sun,
Far athwart his lair I run.

GEORGE DARLEY, "THE UNICORN"

Acknowledgements

The pictures in this book are reproduced with the kind permission of the following libraries:

The Bridgeman Art Library: **front jacket:** Perseus and Andromeda by Peter Paul Reubens, Hermitage, St Petersburg. **front flap:** Pan and the Centaurs *(miniature)*, Biblioteca Medicea-Laurenziana, Florence, K&B News Foto, Florence. **back jacket** and **p7:** St George and the Dragon by Sir Edward Burne-Jones, William Morris Gallery, Walthamstow. **p2** and **p53:** Perseus freeing Andromeda by Piero di Cosimo, Galleria Degli Uffizi, Florence. **p8:** Marriage of Heaven and Hell detail by William Blake, Fitzwilliam Museum, University of Cambridge. **p9:** illustration from The Magic Flute, Austrian School, 18th century. **p12** *(detail, left)*: Lat 9471 f.16r November by the Master of the Rohan Hours, Grandes Heures de Rohan, Biblioteque Nationale, Paris. **p13:** Dead poet borne by Centaur by Gustave Moreau, Musee Gustave Moreau, Paris. **p18:** Polyphemus the Cyclops, Roman mosaic early 4th century, Villa Romana del Casale, Piazza Armerina, Sicily. **p19:** Fr 606 f.11 Ulysses piercing the eye of the Cyclops, from the L'Epitre d'Othea, by the Epitre, Works of Christine de Pisan, Biblioteque Nationale, Paris. **p23:** Medusa Asleep by Fernand Khnopff, F.Labisse Collection, Neuilly. **p26:** *(detail, left)* Griffin and St Thaddeus by Andrea Castagno, San Apollonia, Florence. **p27:** A Chariot with Griffins *(detail)* by Egnazio Danti, Vatican Museums and Galleries, Rome. **p32:** A Race with Mermaids and Tritons by Collier Smithers. **p34:** Attic amphora depicting the struggle between Theseus and the Minotaur, 6th century BC. **p35:** Minotaur by George Frederick Watts, Tate Gallery. **p37:** Hercules Fighting with the Nemean Lion by Francisco de Zurbaran, Prado, Madrid. **p38:** Pegasus, the Winged Horse Ms 35 f.115, Lambeth Palace Library, London. **p41:** Bellerophon Riding Pegasus *(fresco)* by Giovanni-Battista Tiepolo, Palazzo Labia, Venice. **p46:** The Rukh which fed its young on elephants by Edward Julian Detmold, British Library. **p50:** Venus and Mars by Sandro Botticelli, National Gallery, London. **p51:** An Arcadian Landscape with Pan and Syrinx by Jacob de Heusch, Rafael Valls Gallery, London. **p54:** Siren painter: Attic red figure Stamnos, Odysseus & the Sirens. **p55:** The Song of the Sirens by Stuart Davis, Christopher Wood Gallery, London. **p59:** Hercules and the Stymphalian birds by Albrecht Durer, Kunsthistorisches Museum, Vienna. **p60:** The Lady and the Unicorn: 'Sight', c.1500, Musee Cluny, Paris. **p61:** Orpheus Charming the Animals by Jacob Bouttats (fl.c.1675), Rafael Valls Gallery, London.

E.T. Archive: **p1:** Historia Naturalis c1460, Victoria & Albert Museum. **p15:** Cerberus by William Blake, Tate Gallery. **p29:** Canto XIII Here the brute harpies make their nest, from Milton's Paradise Lost illus by Gustave Dore. **p42:** *(detail)* Phoenix arising from flames, Bestiary c.1200, Bodleian Library. **p44:** Pliny the Elder - Historia Naturalis, Sienese c.1460, Phoenix on nest, Victoria and Albert Museum.

Fine Art Photographic: **p49:** In the morning of the world by George Percy Jacomb-Hood.

The Visual Arts Library, London: **p10:** Minerva taming the Centaur by Botticelli, Uffizzi, Florence. **p11:** The fight of the Centaurs by Bocklin, Basel, Kunstmuseum. **p21:** St George and the Dragon by Green, Chris Beetles Gallery. **p24:** Head of Medusa by Caravaggio, Uffizzi, Florence. **p25:** Phineas and his companions turned to stone by Giordano. **p26:** *(detail right)* Griffin from bestiary, Harley ms 4751 f,76, British Museum. **p33:** Mermaids by Bocklin, Basel, Kunstmuseum. **p39:** Poetic Inspiration by Louis Jean Lagrenee. **p43:** Phoenix, 5th century, by Regnault de Montauban, Biblioteque de l'Arsenal, Paris. **p44:** Le livre des Merveilles, illustrated by the Master of Boucicaut and the Master of Bedford, 15th century, Biblioteque Nationale, Paris. **p48:** Nymphs and Satyrs by Caresme. **p56:** The Sphinx by Moreau, private collection. **p57:** Oedipus explaining the enigma to the Sphinx by Ingres, Musee du Louvre, Paris. **p62:** Heures d'Antione le Bon, 1533, Biblioteque Nationale, Paris. **p63:** The Triumph of Castity by pupil of Mantegna, Denver Museum of Art.

Illustrations: **p17:** Bellerophon and the Chimaera by HJ Ford. **p31:** The Jabberwocky by Sir J Tenniel from Alice Through the Looking Glass.